Kathy c Tressl

THIS BOOK OF COMFORT
IS PRESENTED TO

In the time of sorrow
with the sincere prayer
that the enclosed message
will bring help and peace
to you and yours.

Sincerely,

When Loved Ones Are Taken in Death

by
Lehman Strauss

Daybreak Books

Zondervan Publishing House
Grand Rapids, Michigan

Design: Koechel / Peterson, Mpls., Mn.
Cover Photo: Steve and Mary Skjold

Copyright: 1964, This Edition 1973
By Zondervan Publishing House
Grand Rapids, Michigan

Daybreak Books are published by Zondervan
Publishing House, 1415 Lake Drive, S.E.,
Grand Rapids, Michigan 49506

ISBN 0-310-33102-1

Library of Congress Catalog Card Number: 72-95528

Printed in the United States of America

90   91   92   93 / CH / 31   30   29

When Loved Ones Are Taken in Death

The Bible says, "It is appointed unto men once to die" (Hebrews 9:27). We know this and believe it, and we expect that in the normal course of events sooner or later that experience will come to us. Nothing is more certain in life than the fact of death. It is confirmed to us every day we live. We read about it in every daily newspaper. There is death by disease, accident, murder, starvation, drowning. No city newspaper has ever had cause to omit the obituary column.

Vital statistics tell us that the world's population is running close to three billion. Of this number approximately thirty million die every year. Has it ever occurred to you what this means? It means that every second, with every tick of the clock, one person somewhere in the world dies. Every day 86,400 persons die. If each person who died were to leave behind only one sorrowing loved one, there would be added daily to the millions of heavy-hearted men and women 86,400 more to swell the ranks

of the tried and the troubled. Now all of this causes us to stop and think, for the moment at least. But we soon forget it as we enter into the routine of daily work and play.

Then one day the bottom drops out of our world. Death enters our family, taking from us a cherished loved one, possibly a mother or father, son or daughter, husband or wife, or some other relative or friend. Some of us have already had this experience. We said the final good-bye as our loved one departed this life. This is not an easy experience for any of us. The Christian, even though he is well instructed in what the Bible teaches, finds such a trial to be most difficult. We are just never quite prepared for it.

It is my intention in these pages to help you to see what the Christian's attitude toward death, with its accompanying sorrow and bereavement, should be. We dare not look upon this subject as a morbid one to be repressed. On the contrary we need to consider death since we know it is certain. My aim here is to help you to see what is involved for those who are taken from us in death and to grasp something of what God has for us who are left behind. You see, for the Christian, death has its bright side. But I fear that too few of God's children can see that bright side through their veil of tears. The fear and sting of death still abide, even among the best of believers. Though one lives in the warmth of Gospel truth, he feels the chill of death. Possibly this is so because the realm of death is that unfamiliar area not known to the living. We have never experienced that which lies beyond. With all our boasted knowledge it is still the realm of the unknown. It is the interruption of all of life's plans and purposes. It is the severing of relations from those whom we loved and for whom we lived and labored. Death is just not easy to accept. I confess that this was my feeling as I stood by the side of my mother who was about to cross over. I had known many comforting truths taught to me from the Word of God, but my knowledge had never before been put to the test. It has been a theoretical knowledge and not experiential.

Preparation for death must be made in life, whether that death be your own or a loved one dear to you. Most people are unwilling to think seriously about death until it is forced upon them. But sooner or later death is certain to come into the experience of each of us. When it does come, the best course of action is to face it squarely in the light of the Scripture. Surely it is the part of wisdom to be prepared for this new and strange experience.

Death
Is
Certain

The death of your loved one is an experience common to all mankind. We set out on the journey of life with high hopes. These hopes are often built upon plans we have made. We think in terms of our children's needs, their happiness, education and future careers. We plan retirement with our mate in marriage. But one day we are suddenly stopped cold when the icy fingers of death snatch away one of our precious loved ones. Physicians and surgeons, nurses and friends, all have done what they could to save the life, but in the gracious and perfect providence of God, death has conquered. That life is now beyond recall. Nothing in all this world can bring back those whom God has taken in death. And if we believe that our times are in God's hands, and be sure they are, neither you nor I could take to ourselves the responsibility of determining when life on earth should cease for anyone. Death is certain for each of us, and God who lends us life must determine when that moment of death must come.

When I was a pastor in my first church in Pennsylvania, a young mother, not yet forty years old, died suddenly without warning. She was, from all appearances, a normally healthy woman. The physician attributed her death to a heart attack. The woman's husband, while deeply moved and sorely grieved, accepted his wife's passing as a providential act of God. But there were three teen-aged children left behind also. These three precious young people were in confusion wondering why their mother, whom they loved and on whom they depended, was taken from them. It took several weeks of counseling with them in this home before those young folks saw the truth of God's Word, that "it is appointed unto men once to die" (Hebrews 9:27), and that God only can fix the hour of death. Moreover God never acts without reason. When He permits death to take our loved ones, He has a purpose for doing so, and that purpose is always for our good as well as for His glory. We must believe this because it is so. The Bible says, "And we know that all things work together for good to them that love God, to them who are the called according to His purpose" (Romans 8:28). One by one they came to see these things. God, through His Word, had given them light, so that they were able to say with Job, whose seven sons and three daughters were killed, ". . . The LORD gave and the LORD hath taken away; blessed be the name of the LORD" (Job 1:21). They were reconciled to the fact that God makes no mistakes and that He would provide for their future. That incident took place many years ago. Today these young people, now married and raising their own children, have a fuller knowledge of these things. But one day they shall have perfect knowledge when they shall know even as they are known by God Himself.

The fact of universal death must be understood and accepted by us. It is the first step in preparing us for the departure of loved ones. And I might add that it is the first step in getting ourselves ready for our own death. And do any of us know when this will be? "Whereas ye know not what shall be on the morrow. For what is your life? It is even a vapor, that appeareth for a little time, and then vanisheth away. For that ye ought to say, If the Lord will, we shall live, and do this, or that" (James 4:14, 15). We do to ourselves a grave injustice when we leave death out of a day's plans. What is your life? It is a brief thing, a little time; it will soon be gone. Yes, your life is like a little steam issuing from the spout on your teakettle. It is there one moment; gone

the next.

Whatever business fills your day, you had better include the possibility of death. Write down on the day's agenda. "Deo volente" (D.V.), God willing. We are human mortal creatures. The only certain factor about life is that sooner or later it will end in death.

Death Is Sleep

All that can be known about life after death is recorded only in the Bible. Non-Christian religions have fanciful and weird ideas as to what happens after death, but the Word of God only has the true answer. To reject the Word of God is to cast away all true knowledge and all hope. To accept the Word of God is to have the divinely-stated facts, and these provide peace which passes all understanding.

In the New Testament there are different words used to describe the death of a Christian. While they are figures of speech, they convey to us precisely what happens at the moment of death.

First, death is likened to **sleep.** Now this does not have reference to the sleep of the spirit or the soul, but only to the body. The spiritual part of man never lapses into a state of sleep or unconsciousness. Christians of earlier times called their cemeteries "cubicula," which meant sleeping places. Our bodies sleep or rest in the grave until the day of resurrection. When our Lord knew that Lazarus had died, He said to His disciples, "Our friend Lazarus sleepeth; but I go, that I may awake him out of sleep" (John 11:11). The disciples did not understand Christ's figurative use of the word "sleep," and so they replied, "Lord, if he sleep, he shall do well" (vs. 12). "Howbeit Jesus spake of His death: but they thought that He had spoken of taking of rest in sleep. Then said Jesus unto them plainly, Lazarus is dead" (vss. 13,14). Here the words "sleep" and "death" are used interchangeably. When loved ones who are God's children are taken in death, their bodies are said to be asleep, thus we lay the body to rest awaiting the day of resurrection "when this corruptible shall have put on incorruption, and this mortal shall have put on immortality" (1 Corinthians 15:54).

When Stephen, the first recorded martyr of the Christian Church, gave his testimony concerning Christ before the rulers of the synagogue, they set about to kill him. His message aroused their hatred because they were the enemies of Jesus Christ. The inspired record says, "And they stoned Stephen, calling upon God, and saying, Lord Jesus, receive my spirit" (Acts 7:59). This was Stephen's last moment of life on earth. He was God's child with the knowledge that his spirit would go at once to be with his Lord. Christ's last word from the Cross was, "Father, into Thy hands I commend My spirit" (Luke 23:46). Stephen learned from these words of the Lord Jesus that "to be absent from the body" meant "to be present with the Lord" (2 Corinthians 5:8). After Stephen prayed, "Lord Jesus, receive my spirit," Luke writes, "And he kneeled down, and cried with a loud voice, Lord, lay not this sin to their charge. And when he had said this, he fell **asleep**" (Acts 7:60). Literally he died, for death is the separation of man's spirit from his body.

The word of God contains other references in which the death of Christians is expressed in terms of sleep. At least thirteen times the word, "sleep" is used of the death of the body, and always of the death of the believer in Christ (Matthew 27:52; John 11:11; Acts 7:60; 13:36; 1 Corinthians 11:30; 15:6, 8, 51; 1 Thessalonians 4:13, 14, 15; 2 Peter 3:4). That the body alone is in view in this figure of speech is evident, for the word resurrection is used of the body only. The prophet Daniel wrote,

"And many of them that **sleep** in the dust of the earth shall awake, some to everlasting life, and some to shame and everlasting contempt" (Daniel 12:2).

From these several passages in God's Word we gather the comforting and consoling idea that at the moment of death all of life's cares, anxieties, problems, trials, pain and suffering slip away from the child of God forever. Having entered eternity the believer in Christ shall never more remember the ills of this life. "The former shall not be remembered, nor come into mind" (Isaiah 65:17). The sleep of your loved one's body is a blessed release. Rest in this truth!

Death Is A Departure

Another word used in the New Testament for death is **departure.** Paul wrote in his last Epistle, just prior to his death, "For I am now ready to be offered, and the time of my **departure** is at hand" (2 Timothy 4:6). The Greek word used here is **analusis,** and it is used metaphorically in a nautical way as when a vessel pulls up anchor to loose from its moorings and set sail, or in a military

way as when an army breaks encampment to move on. In the ancient Greek world this term was used also for freeing someone from chains, and the severing of a piece of goods from the loom. This is what death is as described in the Bible. Here we are anchored to the hardships and heartaches of this life. In death the gangway is raised, the anchor is weighed and we set sail for the Golden Shore. In death we break camp here to start for Heaven.

I have been away from home many times to minister the Word of God in some distant places. I know of no feeling quite like that which is aroused when the day comes to depart for home. As the hour for flight time approaches, there arises within me a good feeling just to know I am heading home. The great Apostle spoke of his "desire to **depart, and to be with Christ; which is far better**" (Philippians 1:23). Paul wrote these words as a prisoner in a Roman prison. The word was sometimes used of a prisoner when he was released. Now death is an intensely solemn thing, but it can be an inexplainably glorious thing also. It is a release for this mortal body of humiliation; humiliated by failing eyesight, fading beauty, falling hair and a fainting heart. Paul himself says that to **depart** and be with Christ is far better. We should not be anything else than happy in the thought of heading Home. And certainly we should be joyful even in our sorrow when God releases a loved one from this world of woe to take him or her to Himself. To Timothy the separation from Paul will be lacerating. For Paul his own death will be a glorious release, not from the Mamertine dungeon where he penned his final Epistle, but from his ailing, failing body. To depart from this land means that the Christian starts for a better Land.

Isaac Watts expressed this great truth in one of his best hymns —

> There is a Land of pure delight,
> Where saints immortal reign;
> Infinite day excludes the night,
> And pleasures banish pain.

Why should we begrudge our loved ones this final journey when God summons them home? I have come to the conclusion that for the most part we are selfish. We would prevent, if we could, a child of God from passing to his eternal Home. How utterly wrong is such an attitude! My heavenly Father knows when He is ready for me to come Home, so whenever He calls me to **depart,** I trust that my loved ones will rejoice with me. "We are confident, I say, and willing rather to be absent from the

19

body, and to be present (at home) with the Lord" (2 Corinthians 5:8). Heaven is our eternal home. Our Lord is there. All saved persons will be there. So it seems to me that those of us who are going there, and who believe in Heaven, should receive much comfort and inspiration from our faith. The passing of a Christian from this world is not a departure into an unknown world; it is a going to a place prepared for him by the Lord Jesus Christ. Our Saviour said, "I go to prepare a place for you" (John 14:2). He saw to it that the death of His followers was not a venture into a strange and alien atmosphere. True, there is a certain strangeness about death because of the "onceness" of the experience, but we need have no fear if we are trusting Him Who said, "I am the resurrection, and the life: he that believeth in Me, though he were dead, yet shall he live" (John 11:25).

Life in Heaven is neither strange nor unwelcome to our loved ones who have died in the Lord. They are at Home with Him who has redeemed them by His own death on the Cross. Now do not clutch frantically and faithlessly to this fact, but rest in it happily and confidently. When the Christian departs his home on earth, he goes to a better Home in Heaven. When he says farewell to those who love him here, he goes to be with God who loves him with an everlasting love. Death is indeed a delightful departure.

⚘ Death Is ⚘
An Exodus

Another word used to explain death is **exodus,** spelled in Greek exactly as it is in English. In the Authorized (King James) Version of the Bible it appears twice and is translated "decease." It means "a way out" or a "going out."

Our Lord used the word on the Holy Mount when He was transfigured before Moses, Elijah, Peter, James and John. It is recorded that Christ "appeared in glory, and spoke of His decease [**exodus**] which He would accomplish at Jerusalem" (Luke. 9:31). Do not miss an important point here. Our Lord spoke of His "going out" from this life as an accomplishment. By His death something was going to be accomplished, that is, something was to be fulfilled, completed, carried out to the full. We know that it was the fulfillment of the Divine promise of redemption through the sacrifice of His own Blood. His death was to be a "way out" of sin and judgment for the rest of the human race. In other words, His departure would be the means of leading us out of bondage.

This word takes us back to the Book of Exodus where we have the record of God's people "going out" of Egypt. For them it was "a way out" of bondage into liberty, "a way out" of sorrow and hardship into a land flowing with milk and honey. The **exodus** of the children of Israel from Egypt was the turning point in that nation's history. The **exodus** of Christ at Calvary was the turning point in the world's history. It was a mighty accomplishment.

The Apostle Peter used this word when speaking of his own death. He wrote, "yea, I think it meet, as long as I am in this tabernacle, to stir you up by putting you in remembrance; Knowing that shortly I must put off this my tabernacle, even as our Lord Jesus Christ hath showed me. Moreover I will endeavor that ye may be able after my decease [**exodus**] to have these things always in remembrance" (2 Peter 1:13-15). To Peter death was a deliverance from the taskmasters and enslavements of this present life; it was "a way out" from the imperfect to the perfect, from a partial knowledge to complete knowledge, from the old gloom into a new glory. Death for the children of God is an accomplishment.

Peter calls his body a "tabernacle" or a tent. The body at its best is a frail dwelling place for the spirit of man. Like the children of Israel in Egypt, we are pursued by relentless foes, the world, the flesh and the Devil. Weakness, sickness, old age, all pursue hard after us. Beloved child of God, the body in which we live is not as important as the man who lives in the body. We are merely "strangers and pilgrims" here on earth (1 Peter 2:11). One day we too are going to move out of this old tent. The Apostle tells us that it is only proper that he stir us up by putting us in remembrance of these things. It is so easy to become wrapped up in the things of this brief life and in this passing world that we forget our coming **exodus.**

How calmly and assuredly Peter speaks of his death! Though it was to be shameful and painful, he refers to it as his **exodus,** his "way out," and he manifests no fear or consternation. Death to this child of God would be a sweet release. And so he planned his own funeral and prepared a comforting word for the blessing of those who would be left behind until the day of their **exodus.**

This assuring word is for both you and me. We can look forward to the end of life

without fear. Death for each believer will be the sweet release of being "absent from the body" and "at home with the Lord" (2 Corinthians 5:8). Death and the grave are not a blind alley, but a thoroughfare into Heaven itself. Men may talk about the Great Unknown, the Leap into the Dark, the Great Beyond, but such is not the language of God's Word. Death for the Christian is an **exodus,** a way out and a way in, the way out of life's trials and uncertainties and the way into the presence of our blessed Lord and those loved ones who have gone on before.

Heaven Is Real

Since death is a departure, an exodus, a going away, it follows that the souls which have departed this life have gone somewhere.

When I served as a pastor in Eastern United States, I always enjoyed accompanying our departing missionaries to New York where they boarded a huge ocean liner for some distant country in South America, Europe or the East. We would bid one another farewell as the vessel pulled away from the dock. I don't ever remember leaving the dock for my home until the vessel was completely out of sight. And then we would turn to go to our automobiles for the drive back to Pennsylvania. But invariably someone would be heard to say of the missionaries, **"There they go.**" Now no one would question that their departure from New York meant that they would be arriving at some other place at some time. When we are absent from one place we are present at another. Somewhere, at some time, someone will be heard saying, **"Here they come."**

When God calls our believing loved ones from our midst, we say that they have departed. In Heaven they say, "Here they come." The dead are absent from their bodies (and from us) but they are present with the Lord. So wrote the inspired Apostle Paul in Second Corinthians 5:8. Since they are no longer here they are elsewhere. They have been called by God to come to Him. It is divinely written of the departure of Enoch that "God took him" (Genesis 5:24).

Now if you ask where God is, I can assure you that He is some place. He has His abode. Our Lord spoke often of Heaven as the dwelling place of God. When He taught the disciples the principles of a successful prayer life, He told them to recognize two things; the fact of the Fatherhood of God and the fact that Heaven was His dwelling place. He said, "After this manner

26

therefore pray ye: Our Father which art in Heaven" (Matthew 6:9). When Christ was baptized, there came "a voice from **Heaven,** saying, This is My beloved Son, in Whom I am well pleased" (Matthew 3:17.) In the Sermon on the Mount Jesus said, "Glorify your Father which is in Heaven" (Matthew 5:16), "That ye may be the children of your Father which is in **Heaven**" (Matthew 5:45). "Be ye therefore perfect, even as your Father which is in **Heaven** is perfect" (Matthew 5:48). These are but a few of the many references in the Bible which tell us that God is in Heaven.

Heaven is the place from which Jesus came before His Incarnation, for "the Word was with God" (John 1:1). He said, "I came down from **Heaven**" (John 6:38,42). At His Ascension He was "carried up into **Heaven**" (Luke 24:51), "received up into **Heaven**" (Mark 16:19). "The disciples saw Him taken up into **Heaven**" (Acts 1:11). Before His departure from the earth He said, "In My Father's house are many mansions (abiding places): if it were not so, I would have told you. I go to prepare a place for you" (John 14: 1,2). You can see from these Scriptures that Heaven is a place where God the Father, God the Son and God the Holy Spirit dwell, and the same place to which all the redeemed go when departing this life. We have the assuring word from our Lord that He personally is seeing to its readiness when we depart to go and be with Him.

We know that the Christians who left this earth are now in Heaven in the place our Lord has prepared for them. God's Word speaks of the "whole family in **Heaven** and earth" (Ephesians 3:15). This is the family of God, those who became children of God through faith in the Lord Jesus Christ. Some members of the family have gone to their eternal home in Heaven; others of us are still in our temporary and temporal dwellings here on earth. The family is presently separated, but not divided. Some members of the family have been left alone on earth with their tears and sorrows, but we all shall see the day when the whole family will be at Home with each other and forever with the Lord.

We Shall Know Each Other

"Shall we know each other in Heaven?" This question is asked repeatedly by anxious and concerned persons whose loved ones have crossed over. It is a question of compelling interest, even to poets. One has written,

> "Will they meet us, cheer and greet us,
> Those we've loved who've gone
> before?
> Shall we find them at the portals,
> Find our beautiful immortals,
> When we reach the radiant shore?"

I am not certain that in Heaven they will cheer us when we arrive, but I feel confident that there will be recognition. I make this assertion reverently, not recklessly. Death does not mean the utter forgetfulness of earthly friends and loved ones in the Lord. The emptiness and longing in our hearts, the undying memory of those precious loved ones who have departed, will be more than mere buried hopes. "Now I know in part; but then shall I know even as also I am known" (1 Corinthians 13:12). This verse has in it the implication that we shall know each other better in Heaven than on earth. Here our knowledge of each other is partial; in Heaven it will be complete.

In the Old Testament we find the oft repeated statement that a saint who died "was gathered unto his people." This was said of Abraham (Genesis 25:8), Isaac (Genesis 35:29), Jacob (Genesis 49:33), Aaron (Numbers 20:24), Moses (Numbers 27:12,13). Now this statement could not mean merely being buried with their people. Certainly Moses' body was not buried near any of his loved ones (Deuteronomy 34:6), but he was gathered to them in the abode of departed spirits in a blessed recognition and reunion. When David's baby died, he said, "Can I bring him back? I shall go to him, but he shall not return to me" (2 Samuel 12:23). Surely there would be no comfort for David in going to his child whom he would not know. There would be no point in leading a blind man out to behold a sunset, or a deaf man to a musical concert. The Old Testament believers held to the idea of recognition in Heaven.

In the New Testament there is clear teaching in support of heavenly recognition. On the Mount of Transfiguration, where Jesus took Peter, James and John, two men appeared before the four of them. Who were these two? They were not angels or ghosts, but men in bodies recognizable as such. They talked together that day on the Holy Mount so that the three disciples in their earthly, limited vision recognized the two saints from Heaven.

When the rich man died and went to Hell, "he lifted up his eyes, being in torments, and seeth Abraham afar off, and Lazarus in his bosom" (Luke 16:23). Here we have an instance that proves both recognition and remembrance in the future life. If, in the

abode of the lost with its limitations of knowledge and perception, there is feeling for and recognition of loved ones, how much greater will be the affinity and knowledge of our loved ones in the eternal Home of the redeemed!

A Scottish wife asked her dying husband, "Dear, will we know each other in Heaven?" The dying child of God replied, "My darling, do you think that we shall have less sense in Heaven than we have here?" Happy days they will be when the whole family of God is united in Heaven!

"They will meet, smile and greet us,
    Those we've loved who've gone
        before;
We shall find them at the portals,
    Find our beautiful immortals
When we reach the radiant shore."

Now just one final word. If this message has reached anyone who is not saved; let me assure you that there is no hope of Heaven for you in your present state. Death for the unsaved means the final banishment from God and Christian loved ones. Will you right now confess your sins to God and receive the Lord Jesus Christ as your personal Saviour? "For whosoever shall call upon the name of the Lord shall be saved" (Romans 10:13).